Welcome to the third in a series of booklets on contemporary glass beadma
lets will introduce you to a number of the best and most interesting contempora .... in the country. You will get to learn more about them and their work. They will take this chance to share with us some of
their beadmaking secrets as well as some of their favorite tools.

These booklets will also serve as companion documents to my text on glass beadmaking, **More Than You Ever
Wanted To Know About Glass Beadmaking**. That text provides all the basic knowledge on glass beadmaking skills, while these booklets will show you how different artists put these skills into practice. In these adven-
tures into beadmaking, I will assume that you have at least a passing knowledge of glass beadmaking techniques, and will not try to go into all the basics of the craft. Instead, we will focus on how these beadmakers
work their wonders.

For this booklet, I have chosen to give you a glimpse into the work of another of my favorite beadmaking artists,
Jim Smircich. After seeing some of his work, I am sure that you will understand why.

Artist Bio

Jim Smircich lives in Jasper, Oregon, which is
just a stones throw from Eugene, with his dog
Sally. This country setting with its rolling landscape and distant forested hills provides him an
inspirational view from his workbench. His
lampworking studio is a thirteen-foot camping
trailer that he has renovated and parked near
his house. This relaxing country environment is
quite different from his San Francisco roots. It
allows him to more fully concentrate on his
beadmaking and provides him with endless
hours of quiet repose. For those with the time to
visit him there, he teaches occasional one-on-
one classes.

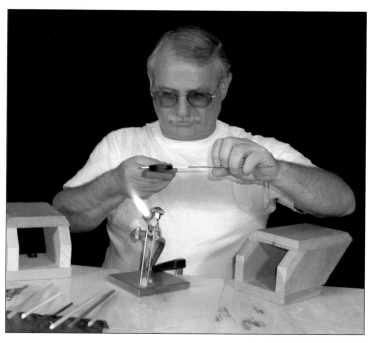

Jim has been interested in art and has been
making his living in it as far back as he can
remember. His commercial art ventures started
at sixteen and a half, when he sculpted wood
figureheads and Tiki gods as an arts and crafts counselor at a summer camp. Since one of these was a pendant, you could probably also say this was when he started out in beadmaking. You can see this early bead,
dated 7/6/59, to the left alongside one of his current masterpieces.

An important experience in Jim's life occurred when he and a friend hitchhiked around Europe after high school.
He ended up spending the last six weeks of the trip in Greece. Because the weather was not the greatest, he
spent many of these days in the National Museum in Athens. He was fascinated with the ancient Greek culture
and especially its art. The geometric patterns on the pottery affected him deeply and he believes that some of
them flow out through him onto his beads. The colors that he uses, especially the blacks, reds, and creams,
echo the colors of that culture.

When it came time to go to college, Jim enrolled in City College of San Francisco and majored in photography.
He soon started working as a freelance photographer in the late 60's and early 70's covering the flowering Rock
and Roll scene. His close friend, Paul Kantner, who had just arrived in San Francisco and was in the process
of forming the rock group Jefferson Airplane, helped influence him in this direction. Jim took photographs for a
number of album covers, posters and songbooks. Besides Jefferson Airplane, he also worked with Quicksilver,
and took one of the classic pictures of Jimi Hendricks that was published in Rolling Stone Magazine. What Jim
really wanted was to do landscape photography like Ansel Adams or Edward Weston, but this dream never
materialized. So, burned out by all the Rock and Roll egos, he was ready for something new.

Then the opportunity arose for Jim to apprentice at Nourot Glass Studios in Benicia, California. He was lucky enough to get this dream job through a friend who worked in the front office and introduced him to the owner, Mike Nourot. This occurred on a weekend fishing trip where they got to discussing glass, and Mike hired him. It was great. Jim likens it to turning a corner and finding yourself in Dorothy's Oz. It was a classic apprenticeship, where he advanced through and learned the different components of the trade. He started out learning to mix glass batch from the raw materials and melting it in a furnace. He also learned to cold work the finishing touches on blown glass objects, and to assist the glassblowers. During those three years he was also tutored in the general art of off-hand glassblowing. He learned to make paperweights, goblets, and vases, as well as to assemble and pull complex glass canes. Unfortunately, a few years later he ended up getting laid off due to a downturn in the economy, but even so he says that he owes an enormous debt of gratitude to Michael Nourot for opening the door into the world of hot glass for him.

After this, Jim went to work with another local glass artist, putting his cane construction skills to use by helping to construct latticino marbles. He spent about three years at this studio, and during this time Jim figures he must have made at least ten thousand marbles.

By 1988 Jim was ready to strike out on his own as a freelance borosilicate lampworker. He bought a torch and messed around with it for about a month before meeting Ann Miller of Ann Miller Wearable Glass (now called Xeno Glass). After seeing her product line, he was confident that he could make her glass components, and got the contract. He produced a multitude of small component parts that she used in making her jewelry. This was a good working relationship that continued for a decade. During that time Jim estimates that he produced over a hundred thousand borosilicate jewelry components. Now that's what I call production.

Four years later, Jim became interested in glass beadmaking through his friend, Art Seymour. After a little experimentation, Art told Jim "that he was a beadmaker but just didn't know it yet." Boy was he right! Jim was hooked and six months later when Art called to tell him of an upcoming bead show, Jim was ready with work to send in for jurying. He was invited to participate in the show at the Bead Museum in Prescott, Arizona (which has since moved to Glendale, Arizona). This show initiated the founding of the Society of Glass Beadmakers (which recently changed its name to the International Society of Glass Beadmakers) and is considered to be its first "Gathering." He was elected the Society's first West Coast regional director and helped to produce the first preplanned Gathering the following year in San Francisco, which is where I met him for the first time.

Since then Jim's fame and skills as a beadmaker have continued to grow. He is known for his classic torpedo shaped beads with dynamic color schemes, some of which harken back to the vibrant tie-dye heritage of the 60's. He is also known for beads that have the appearance of curdling on their surface. He has a number of signature creations that are uniquely his. These include a goddess bead that greatly resembles objects recovered from prehistoric sites, as well as shield shaped pendants and buttons. His works have a simplicity that also appeals to men.

Jim is fascinated by the unexpected. When something strange happens with the glass during the construction of a bead, instead of tossing the bead and moving on, he studies it to discover what happened. His natural curiosity leads him to play with these changes to see what he can do with them. He believes that each of these experiences is like a door that may be hiding something wondrous. He developed his black web effect and the amazing stone-like beads that he can create with it when following up on the formation of some scum on an opalino glass bead.

Among his fellow beadmakers, Jim is renowned for his ability to make finely shaped beads using a minimum of tools. He makes use of his knowledge of heat control and gravity to shape the majority of his beads. He has experimented extensively with mixing colors, some of which achieve startling effects because they are not truly compatible. He has also done considerable work with the fuming of metals on his beads to apply enchanting earthy colors. Along with this he has developed a relaxing work style that as we will see minimizes any muscle strain to the arms, shoulders and back, allowing longer work sessions at the torch without adverse effects.

So enough talk. Let's let some of his beads do the talking. Examine these fine creations on the next few pages and then we will discuss some of the techniques he uses.

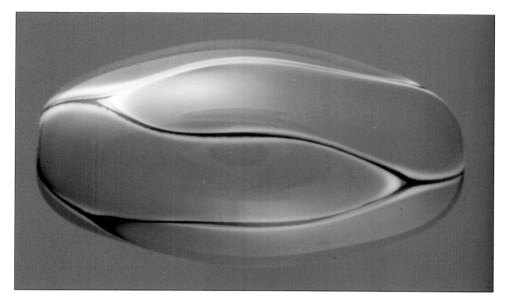

Left:
Interlaced Stripe
Bead, 1993
Photo by:
Mike Rachoff

Right:
Wavy Ended
Flower Bead, 1995
Photo by:
Mike Rachoff

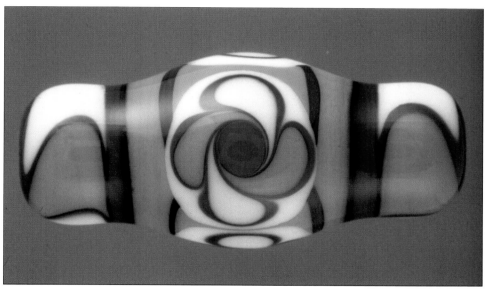

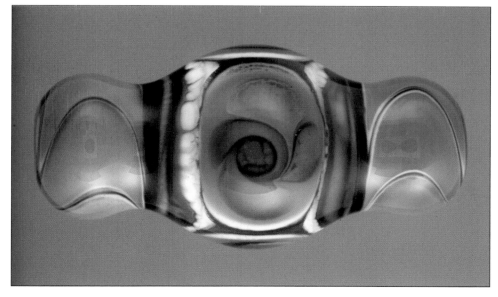

Left:
Wavy Ended
Flower Bead, 1995
Photo by:
Mike Rachoff

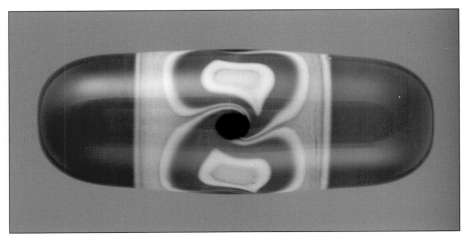

Left:
Twisted Dot Chain
Bead, 1995
Photo by:
Mike Rachoff

Right:
Multi-Stage Wave
Bead, 1995
Photo by:
Mike Rachoff

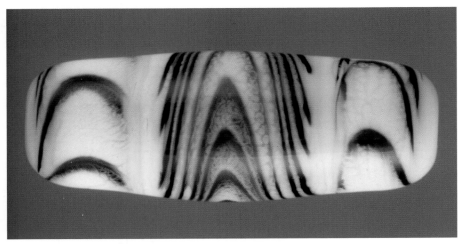

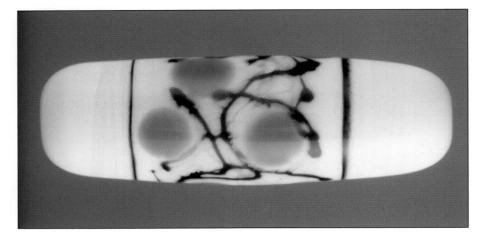

Left:
Random Thread
Bead, 1995
Photo by:
Mike Rachoff

Right:
Script Signature Bead
2001 Demo Bead

Left:
Spot and Dot
Bead with
Pinwheels, 1995
Photo by:
Mike Rachoff

Right:
Wavy Ended
Pinwheel Bead,
1995
Photo by:
Mike Rachoff

Left:
Eye Bead, 1997

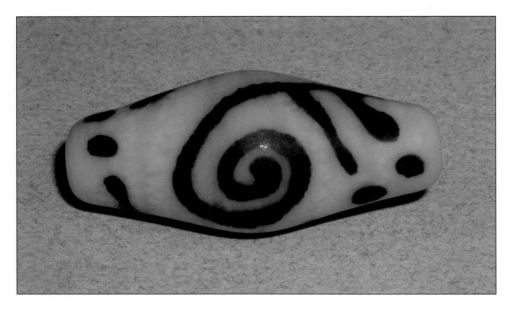

Left:
Tumbled Petroglyph
Bead, 1997

Right:
Twisted Cased
Cane Bead, 1998

Left:
Rune Bead, 1997

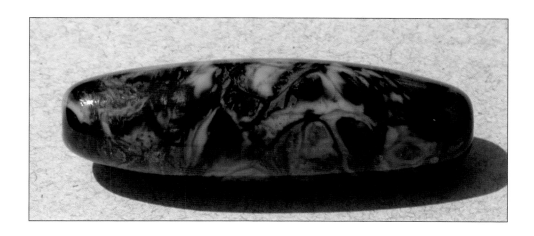

Left:
Black Lace Bead,
2001

Right:
Black Web Bead,
2001

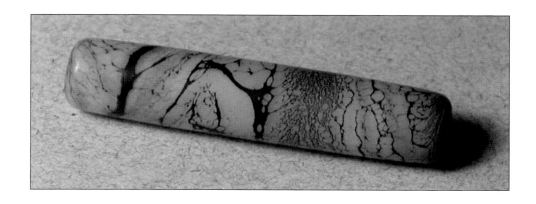

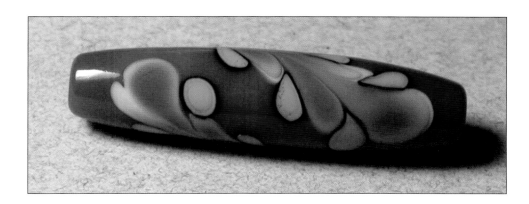

Left:
Combed Floret
Bead, 2001

Right:
Classic Black Web
Bead, 2001

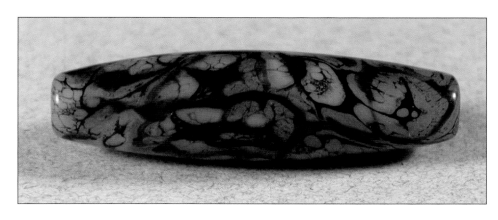

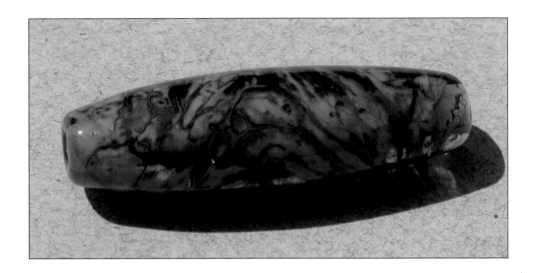

Left:
Black Lace Bead,
2001

Right:
Black Lace Melon
Bead, 2001

Left:
Black Lace Bead,
2001

Now that you have seen a collection of Jim's beads, let's discuss how he goes about making some of them. To understand how he is able to control the flow of glass to get such smooth fluid shapes with minimum tooling, you have to understand the properties of hot glass.

Properties of hot glass

At room temperature and well above, glass is a hard brittle solid, but as you get it hotter, it becomes more and more fluid. As it does so, it will no longer keep its shape and will start to flow. Its shape will now be dictated by a new set of rules:

1.   Surface tension will try to gather it into a ball.
2.   Gravity causes it to run downhill.
3.   The hotter it is the faster it flows.

To see an example of these rules in action, take a glass rod and heat it up in a flame. When you begin, the edges on the end of the rod are sharp as in the top figure to the right. As you heat it up hot enough to start melting, surface tension will start to round or smooth out the edges as in the second picture. As you get a little more of the glass molten, surface tension will form a small ball of molten glass on the end of the rod. But as you start adding more molten glass, this ball will start to droop under the influence of gravity as in the fourth picture. If you rotate the rod on its axis, you can prevent the droop because the glass will not have time to flow. By continuing to play with this process, you will discover that as the glass gets hotter you will have to rotate the rod faster to keep the ball balanced on the end and to keep it from drooping. This is because the glass is getting more fluid. Also as the ball gets larger, you have to turn faster because the effect of gravity becomes more pronounced with the larger mass of glass.

So the more glass that you have molten and the hotter it is, the harder it will be to control. It will try to run away from you. Therefore, to tame this wild glass you need to learn to control its temperature. This involves learning when and how to apply heat as well as learning to read the temperature and depth of heat in a bead.
· When you want to shape the bead, it needs to be molten to the core.
· When working on surface decorations, you only want the outer surface molten.
(Here we are using the term molten to mean hot enough for the glass to flow.)

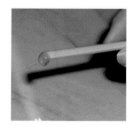

As an example of how glass can flow under the application of heat, look at the series of photos at the bottom of this page. In this series, Jim changes a basic torpedo-shaped bead at the left into a small vessel shape by heating up the center section of the bead and tilting the mandrel down to the left. This causes much of the glass in the body of the bead to flow downhill to become the body of the vessel. It is mesmerizing to watch him move the glass around like this. With this technique, he can also achieve a number of other interesting bead shapes. These include the "knuckle bone" which has a bulge in the center of the bead and the "apple core" which is narrow in the center and thicker at the ends.

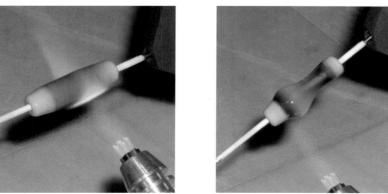

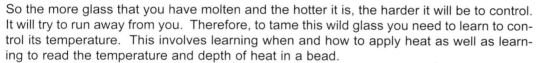

Degree and Depth of Heat

One of Jim's special skills is his understanding and control of heat. The two main considerations in heat control are:

- Degree of Heat - How hot a certain location on the bead is.

- Depth of Heat - What is the distribution of the heat in the bead.

The degree of heat can be monitored by visually assessing the color of the light that is radiating off a bead. The hottest color is yellow. As the bead cools, it will go through the colors of orange, and various shades of red until it reaches the hot glass color for the glass. As an example of this, examine the series of photos below where a round periwinkle blue bead cools from yellow, to orange, to medium red, to low red and finally back to periwinkle blue. The hot glass color can vary tremendously among different glasses: white turns clear; yellow turns red, red turns black, etc.

 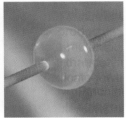   

You can see the difference in temperature in the photos above. Along with the temperature change, the glass in the bead is going through corresponding changes in fluidity. The hotter the bead is, the easier the glass flows. For different beadmaking operations you will want the glass at different temperatures. For gross glass movement or to allow surface tension to round up a bead, you will have to be at yellow to high orange heat. To attach a punty for surface distortion or stretching, you want to be at high or medium red heat. To distort a surface or to pull a cane, you wait until the glass cools to medium or low red heat.

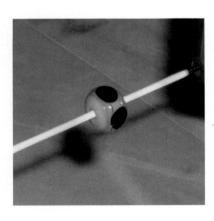 In order to control how much of the bead you affect, you also want to control the depth of heat. Sometimes you only want to heat up the surface of the bead. Other times you want to heat it up to the core. You will often hear these referred to as surface and core heat, and they have very different effects. For example, when you are melting in surface decorations like dots, most of the time you will want to retain the size and shape of the dots as they are melted into the bead surface, as shown in the picture to the left. Here you proceed by just heating the tops of the  dots as you hold the surface of the bead so that it is just barely touching the bottom of the flame. If instead you hold the whole bead in the flame, the core will get hot also and can move around, distorting the dots as seen in the picture to the right. As you will soon come to see, this technique can also be done on purpose to make a wavy bead.

Another thing that you will hear mentioned in discussions of heat control are terms that define how much of the bead you are heating up. You may heat up the whole bead, the center, an end, or some smaller amount. You may apply a line of heat to rake a location, or only a splash of heat to one small spot to twist it. These are all terms that are used to describe controlled application of heat.

Applying glass to form a bead

Let's start with the basics and look at Jim's techniques for laying down glass onto a mandrel to form a bead.

Round beads

Most novice beadmakers learn to make a round bead by touching a ball of molten glass on the end of a rod onto the mandrel and then quickly rotating the mandrel to trail the glass around it. This invariably ends up with a

bead that varies in width around the mandrel, as seen to the left. Novices do this because they have not learned to be comfortable with hot glass and do not know how to achieve uniform application of heat.

Jim instead heats the end of a glass rod until it is glowing bright red but has not yet begun to ball up. He then touches this glass to the top of his mandrel and slowly rotates the top of the mandrel away from him while adding more glass. This technique produces a uniform wrap around the mandrel, resulting in a pea bead as in the figure to the right. The problem that most novices have with this technique is where they are applying the flame. Because they are looking down through the flame, they have a hard time judging where the bead or mandrel is in relationship to the flame.

The correct position is to have the bead or mandrel just skirting the bottom of the flame, as in the first five figures below, and not directly in the flame, as in the last figure. The reason for this is that hot glass always flows from a hotter object to the cooler one. Thus in the first five figures, the flame is on the glass rod. This makes it hotter, and causes glass to flow onto the cooler bead or mandrel. In the last figure, the flame is on the bead, and the cooler rod will pull glass off of the bead or mix up the glass in the bead. So you need to learn to tell where you are in the flame. The way to do that is to watch what is glowing as you are applying glass. If the bead or mandrel is glowing then you are too high up in the flame. If the rod is glowing right at the point where it is touching the bead then you are just right. Jim calls this the elbow and if you get good at directing the flame onto this point when making a bead, then you will not need to rotate the feed rod.

After making a few wraps, Jim stops and lets the glass set up into a pea bead. Next he winds extra glass onto the pea bead, forming a disk around it like Saturn, until he has the desired amount of glass for the final bead volume. Then he collapses this disk into a round bead. Again, instead of blasting the flame into the center of the bead, he directs it onto the outer edge of the disk. If you keep doing this as you rotate the bead, the outer edge will start to gather up the glass and develop a rounded edge from surface tension and will look like a bike tire. By heating just the edge, your bead cross section will progress in the manner illustrated in the photos below, until you end up with that perfect round bead with nice puckered ends. Stop heating then.

If you continued to heat the bead, the core would get hot enough that the glass would start to wick out onto the mandrel, creating sharp ends. These would have to be ground off because they can cut bead strings. Let the bead set up a bit before adding decorations and then reheat just its outer surface and not the core, as you add the decorations. After adding all your decorations, you may have to heat the bead enough to let surface tension round it back up for you, but not so much as to induce wicking.

Long Beads

The secret to making a long bead is in establishing good puckered ends at the start. Jim does this by dwelling at both ends of the bead as he wraps the glass onto the mandrel. Another thing that Jim preaches is to apply the glass hotter than taught by most other teachers.

Jim starts out, as before, by getting the end of the rod hot but not balling up, and then applying it to the mandrel. He takes a few wraps around the mandrel at one location to establish a good end for the bead. But since he is making a longer bead, he starts to move the rod to the right applying more glass to the mandrel, as in the photos to the upper left.

As you apply glass, you want the flame directed at the elbow to flow the glass onto the bead smoothly, as shown in the second photo. This is achieved by keeping the bead just below the flame and correctly aiming the flame. If you have your bead too far beneath the flame, the glass that you apply will go onto the bead looking like a rope. This is not desired because it can trap air between wraps.

When Jim gets to the location where he wants the bead to end, he stops moving down the length and makes a couple of wraps around the mandrel at this location to establish a nice uniform end before burning off. He then goes back and adds extra glass to build up the mass of the bead.

To shape the end of a bead, Jim heats the end and tilts that end of the mandrel down slightly to get the glass to flow down the bead to form a water balloon-like shape. Then he brings the bead out of the flame and lets it rest a second above the paddle, maintaining a slight downward tilt and rotation of the mandrel, before touching it to the paddle. His first roll across the paddle is very light and serves to just slightly chill the surface of the bead. He then takes a second pass down the paddle applying pressure as necessary to shape the glass, usually tilting the bead slightly to form one end of a torpedo bead.

He then repeats the process on the other end of the bead. For the center, he starts by heating it to core yellow heat. Then he rocks the bead slightly while the center is still fluid to evenly distribute the glass. When the bead cools to red heat, he shapes the center rocking the paddle to get a nice smooth torpedo shape. Jim advocates that you always establish a smooth bead shape before adding decorations, because then you do not have to distort the decoration to regain the desired bead shape.

When the bead is complete, Jim finishes it off with a fire polishing. This gives the bead a really good shine and removes any chill marks that may have been put into the surface of the bead by shaping it on a paddle.

Wavy Bead

Now that we understand how to make that perfect long bead shape let's discuss some ways that it might be decorated. The first demonstration is a wavy bead. This is a long bead that ends up with lines that form waves on the surface of the bead. Some artists would do this by raking the lines on the bead surface, but Jim does it by using heat control and gravity.

First you apply stripes of glass to the outside of the long bead. Jim does this a little differently then some artists. Instead of going down through the flame to apply the heat, he holds the bead sideways alongside the flame as in the first photo to the left. Then he applies the stripe to the bead by going sideways through the flame, because it is easier to see what he is doing. He heats up the end of the rod and touches it to the far end of the bead. He draws the stripe down the bead by drawing the rod toward him while directing the flame on the joint between the rod and the bead. Jim will usually add at least two or three equally spaced stripes axially down the length of the bead.

Now that he has the stripes in place, Jim heats up only one end of the bead to core heat. When the end of the bead is completely molten, he slows down the rotation of the mandrel so that the glass starts to flow slightly, but not so much that the bead droops too drastically and gets out of control. Soon the stripes will start to spiral around the circumference of the bead. When it gets to the point where he wants it, he brings the spinning bead out of the flame and lets the hot end of the bead set up, freezing the spiral in place. This process is seen in the four photos to the left.

This same process is then repeated to add spirals on the other end of the bead, as in the top two photos on the right, and finally done in the center of the bead, as seen in the photo series to the right. After he has all the waves in place, Jim goes back and reestablishes the smooth shape of the bead. He uses the same process as was used to shape the basic long bead and since he had a well-shaped bead before he started decorating, the bead shape is easier to reestablish.

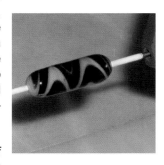

So again during the final bead shaping, he gets one end of the bead hot and tilts the bead slightly to get the glass back out to the end. Then he brings it out of the flame, hesitates slightly while rotating the mandrel, chills the surface of the bead on the paddle, and then paddles the bead to shape. After repeating this on the other end of the bead and in the center he has achieved the finished wavy bead seen to the bottom right. With a final fire polishing, the bead is done and is popped into the annealer.

Black Lace Bead

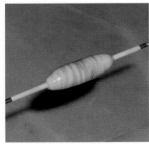

Another easy long bead is Jim's black lace bead. This bead makes use of the fact that Effetre intense black breaks down in an oxidizing flame and separates, leaving interesting rock-like striations on the surface of the bead.

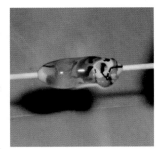

To make this bead, Jim first pulls some fine threads of intense black. This is not the regular Effetre black but a much stronger one. To do this, he heats up the end of an intense black stringer to gather a small ball of glass, and then pulls a fine thread out of it. He pulls two or three of these threads and sets them aside for later.

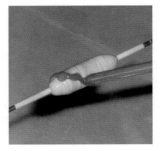

Next Jim makes a long smooth bead blank out of ivory using the techniques discussed earlier. To this blank he adds some dabs of light gray and periwinkle blue as seen in the next two photos to the left. He dabs these colors on lightly, only trying to cover about 20 to 30% of the bead surface while at the same time trying to get a good distribution of color over the surface of the bead.

At this point, Jim adds the intense black thread. He does this by squiggling it on in the outer reaches of his flame. He tries to randomly squiggle it all over the surface of the bead but contends that you should still have good control over the process. You should almost be able to write your name on the bead, as he has done on the demo bead seen in the gallery earlier.

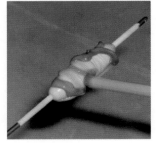

Once he has applied his intense black thread randomly but uniformly over the surface of the bead, he adds more oxygen to his flame to make it slightly oxidizing, as seen in the lower left photo. The tongues of color at the tip of the torch will become equal and shorter, and the torch will sound a little hissy.

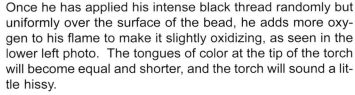

He heats up the bead in this flame to core heat, to decompose the intense black on the surface of the bead. You can see this happening in the series of photos to the right. In the first photo, the bead is just starting to melt and the intense black lines are still solid. At this point he is working any loose threads down onto the surface of the bead so that they remain thread-like instead of balling up. You can also see how the threads spread out somewhat on the surface of the bead and get wider as they melt into the surface.

In the second photo, the whole bead is starting to get molten and you see the glass starting to be pulled into the center by surface tension. The threads are still distinct at this point and have not yet started to break down.

By the third photo, most of the glass is now sucked into the center of the bead and if you look closely the threads have started to break down. This means that the individual

threads break up into multiple narrow lines, which may also be discontinuous. To allow you to better see what this looks like, Jim allows the bead to cool somewhat in the last two photos on the previous page.

At this point some beadmakers might be appalled because all the glass is in the center of the bead and the ends are quite sharp. This is not the shape that you'd want for a finished bead and many would have a hard time recovering a nice bead out of this, but not Jim. Here is where Jim's amazing control of heat comes into play. He starts his recovery by heating up the left side of the bead, as seen in the upper left photo on this page.

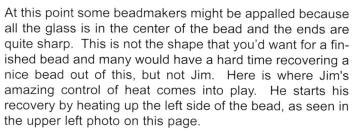

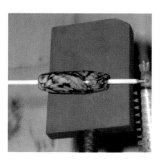

What you may not be able to see very well in the first two photos is that he has also tilted the left end of the mandrel down slightly. Therefore as the glass in that half of the bead starts to melt, it begins to flow back into the left end of the bead because it is flowing downhill. The bead does not droop and stays on center because Jim is rotating the mandrel during this whole process.

After he gets the nice water balloon shape on the end of the bead, he marvers the end to give it a taper and a nice pucker. He does this as before by first removing the bead from the flame, by pausing slightly over the paddle while continuing to rotate the tilted mandrel, by making a first roll down the paddle to slightly chill the bead surface and then applying just enough pressure as he continues to roll the end into shape on the paddle. To get a taper, he has to tilt the mandrel down to the left relative to the paddle as he does this.

Then he repeats this whole process on the other end of the bead to get the basic torpedo shape, as seen in the next three photos. He next smoothes out the arc in the center by core heating this area, rocking the bead slightly to distribute the glass, and allowing it to cool to red heat before paddling it to finish smoothing this area out. If necessary he will repeat any and all of these operations until the shape of the bead is perfect.

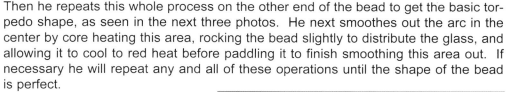

Then Jim goes back into the flame to fire polish any chill marks on the bead surface so that it really shines. Here he only gets the surface of the bead molten and not the core so that he does not lose the perfect shape that he has worked so hard to get. At the same time, he is flame annealing the bead to get as much stress out of it as possible.

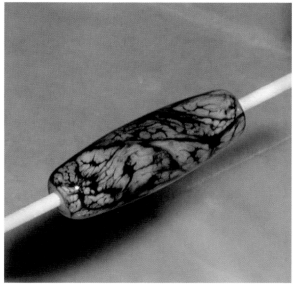

When all this is done, he has the beautiful finished bead seen to the right.

Black Web Bead

The black web bead that Jim demonstrates next looks similar to the black lace bead but it is the result of a reduction reaction of metal oxides in opalino glass. Here the use of a highly reducing flame causes the metal oxides to change into a metal on the surface of the bead.

Jim starts by winding a long bead out of yellow opalino glass and adds some random splotches of dark green opalino. He rarely uses other opalino colors because of compatibility problems. Next he scribbles on the bead with about ten inches of fine black thread, not intense black as in the last example. He only uses a very small amount of this glass because it is not really compatible with opalino glass and if you add too much, it could cause the final bead to crack. He adds the black glass for two reasons. The first is to add just a tinge of purple to the bead, but the most important reason is that this layer will spread over the surface of the bead like oil on water, causing the reduced metallic film on the surface to concentrate into a thicker, more noticeable web.

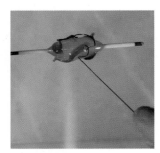

Next Jim cooks this bead to core heat with a very hot reducing flame, to reduce the metal oxides. You can see how reducing this flame is by observing the length of the center yellow tongue coming off the torch in relationship to the cluster of tongues around it. He cooks the bead in this flame until it forms a thick black film all over the surface of the bead. You can also see how all the glass has flowed into the center of the bead as before.

At this point, Jim switches back to a neutral flame (see the even length of the yellow tongues at the end of the torch) and burns some of the black off of the bead surface. At the same time, he is reforming the shape of the bead. He does this by tilting the end of the bead that he is heating downward slightly. This causes glass to flow out of the center of the bead and back into the ends in order to regain that bulging water balloon shape.

With the glass back in the end of the bead, he can now reshape the end as was explained for the last bead. He lifts the bead out of the flame, hesitates for a few seconds rotating over the paddle until it drops to middle red heat, then he lightly rolls it on the paddle to chill the surface and then presses down slightly as he finishes the shaping of the bead end.

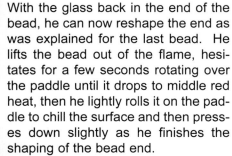

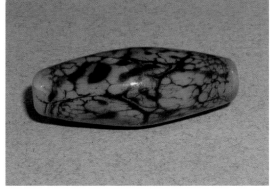

He repeats this process on the other end of the bead and then in the center, rocking the paddle here to give a smooth arc to the bead surface. At this point, you can see the prominent dark web across the surface. After the bead is annealed in the kiln the yellow and green background becomes more vibrant, as seen in the last photo.

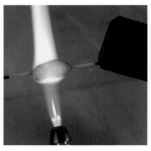

Tools

Jim has some tools that he uses in his work that are a little different than those used by other beadmakers. Let's look at each of these and briefly discuss their use.

To the left of the picture is a Smircich button masher. This is a set of mashers where the length of one of the flat jaws is shorter than the other. This modification allows him to push the shorter jaw up against the rod in mashing out a disk to form a button, while the longer jaw pushes down on the top of the button.

Next is a bow caliper. This tool allows him to compare the diameters of two beads. You adjust it by squeezing in the bow and rotating the knurled nut on the left to hold it in place. He uses it in the construction of his black-ended beads. You can usually find bow calipers at most larger hardware stores.

The tool in the middle is a drafter's compass with two pencil leads. Jim has replaced the pin that is normally on one end of the compass with a second pencil lead. He uses this tool to mark his bead release for the length of a bead. The marks are for orientation only, and they burn off in the flame as he adds glass to the mandrel.

Next is a tweezers-pick combination that Jim put together by wiring a pick to his tweezers. This puts both tools close at hand. He uses this combination tool when forming the shanks on a button or adding loops on his goddess pendants. They allow him to grab or shape with ease.

To the far right of the photo is a set of tile nippers. He uses these to make the indentation between the legs of his goddess pendant. Since the blades do not come together, they do not completely cut through the glass.

At the bottom of the photo is a small dental spatula. Jim uses this tool to put the linear indentations into his melon beads. It is small and easy to handle, and because it does not have much mass, it will not pull a lot of heat out of a bead as he works it.

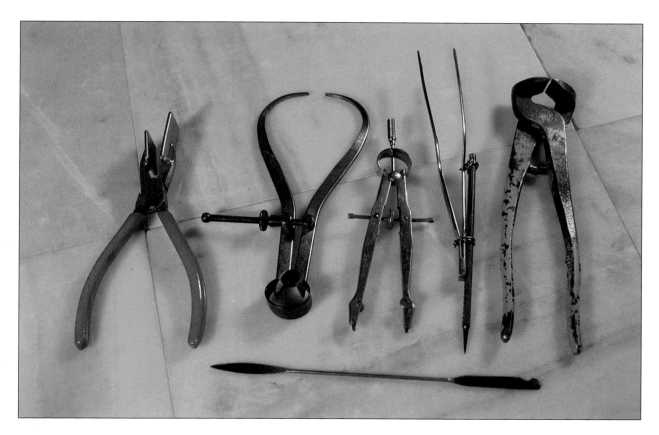

Work Style

Jim has a work style that differs from that of many other beadmakers. Since he tends to make long smooth beads with cylindrical cross sections, he spends a lot of time at the torch rotating his beads in the flame. To make this process easier, he has developed his own unique techniques.

The first thing that he did was to make armrests for his workstation. They are five inches high and have a platform that is about six by four inches to rest his arms on. They take the strain off of his shoulders while he is working. The armrests are clamped to the worktable so that they do not get bumped. Because the sides are shaped like parallelograms, they can be positioned one way or the other to make the resting surface closer or further from his elbow, where he wants the support.

In addition, he has modified his graphite paddle to help support the far end of the mandrel. He sands a little notch about one-half an inch long out of the corner with sandpaper. Then he makes a little indent into the center of this surface with his pick. Once he has a small indent, he takes a ¼" drill bit and drills into the indent turning the drill bit by hand. This gives him more control than trying to use a power drill. Once the drill goes deep enough that he starts to form a cylindrical side on the hole, he stops.

Then when he is working at the torch, Jim has his arms comfortably supported by the armrests and the bead end of his mandrel supported in the drill hole. He turns the mandrel on the other end. In order not to crumble bead release at the end of the mandrel, he pinches the wet release off of the last ¼" of his mandrels as he dips them. This leaves the bare ends of the mandrel exposed free to rotate in the drill hollow in the paddle without disturbing the bead release.

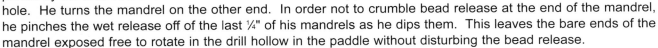

Melon Bead

Jim calls this bead a melon bead because it has exterior ribbing like that can be found on many melons, such as a cantaloupe. These indentations, or ribs, are pushed into the surface of the bead with his dental spatula. The effect is best on cased beads where it causes variations in the magnification of the inside core of the bead.

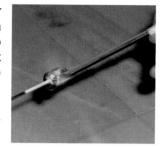

To give the interior of this melon bead some interesting features, Jim starts out with an opaque core, in this case white, as seen in the first photo to the left. To this he adds some interesting color texture by stippling the white core with a couple of other opaque colors. In the next two photos, you can see him adding light lapis blue, red, and yellow stippling.

By stippling, he means rapidly dotting randomly over the surface of the bead without bothering to burn off the fine threads. As he dots, the threads coming off of the dots lift up and fall over onto the surface of the bead. You can see this happening in the third photo and the finished result in the fourth. In the bottom left photo, he is warming the bead and melting in the stippling and reestablishing the smooth surface of the bead.

With the random colors applied, he next cases this core with a light transparent color. When casing, you need to apply the casing glass hot enough so that it flows over the surface of the bead while at the same time keeping the core of the bead cool enough that it does not distort the stippled surface. You also try to apply a uniform thickness of casing so that the core does not look off center. When this is done, Jim establishes a nice oval shape to the bead before continuing.

He finishes up the casing in the second photo to the right, and shapes the cased bead on his paddle in the third. In this photo you can see that even a master can sometimes have problems as the cased stippling has become slightly distorted. Notice the length to diameter ratio of this bead. Melon beads look best with a fairly large diameter. Jim usually shoots for a length-to-diameter ratio of about 3 to 2.

Now it is time to start putting the indentations into the surface of the bead. Jim starts by putting a line of heat at one location around the bead, as in the second photo from the bottom, and then he presses his spatula in at this point parallel to the axis of the bead, as in the bottom photo.

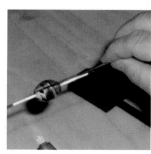

To complete the indentation, he splashes some heat between the end of the indentation and the mandrel. He then extends the indentation into this splash by inserting the spatula into the part of the indentation that is still hard and rocking it up toward the mandrel as in the first picture

to the left on the next page. He does not go all the way to the mandrel because he wants to keep smooth ends and does not want to risk cutting into his bead release. Then he does the same thing on the other end of the indentation as seen in the second photo to the left.

On the second indentation, Jim wants to be sure that it ends up exactly opposite the first one. To ensure that this happens, he puts a small splash of heat approximately where he thinks that this indentation should be and points the end of the bead toward himself so that he can precisely mark the location by lightly pressing into the surface with his spatula.

Then he reheats this marked area with a line of heat and works in the center section of that indentation by pressing the spatula deeper into the bead. He follows this up by extending the indentation on both ends as before. This idea of pointing the bead toward you is useful, and will allow you to precisely place all sorts of other types of surface decorations.

Jim repeats this whole process for the third and fourth indentations, continuing to point the end of the bead towards himself to precisely place the mark before really pressing into the surface. After that point, he no longer needs to point the bead at himself because he can see the two indentations that he is trying to place the crease between.

In doing the remaining creases, he works one side of the bead and then the exact opposite side around the circumference. This avoids heating one side of the bead so much that the heat softens the sharpness of the indentations. This is also a good general practice to use with raised decorations too.

Finally all eight indentations are in place. Jim generally stops at this point because it becomes harder to add new indentations without softening adjacent ones, because of their close proximity, and eight indentations create a good visual appearance to the bead.

You can see the finished melon bead to the right. The secret to making this bead is in getting the indentations equally spaced around the circumference. If they are not, the bead just doesn't look right.

Color Mixing

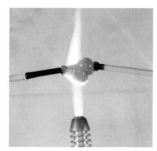

Never satisfied with the Effetre color palette and always trying to develop new tricks, Jim likes to mix different colored glasses together to make new ones. In the past this has included mixing incompatible opalino glass with the regular Effetre colors to get his curdling effect. He does not teach that effect any more because it was very tricky and many students ended up with cracked beads caused by adding too much of the mix to the bead.

When you mix colors together, you are never quite sure what color will result because you are not really mixing pigments but metal oxides, which can interact with each other. As an example, in the demonstration on this page Jim mixes opaque periwinkle blue with dark transparent purple. Most people would expect that this would end up with an opaque color or possibly a translucent one, but instead he gets a transparent purple blue.

In preparing to mix colors, Jim bundles together equal lengths of the rods and canes that he wants to mix. He controls the mix formula by the size and number of each colored rod that he adds. Here he is mixing two colored rods of equal diameter together, so this is a fifty-fifty mix. Jim usually uses pieces about six inches long, but inexperienced beadmakers may want to restrict themselves to more manageable lengths.

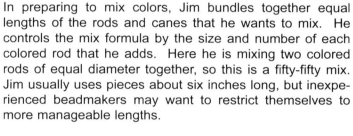

When he is ready to start mixing, Jim heats the ends of the components and puntys them onto a rod about nine inches long, which will act as a handle, as seen in the first two photos on the left. He lets this joint set up before continuing. Then he attaches another handle on the other end.

To begin mixing, Jim heats up the bundle just to the left of the right handle. You do not want to get any of the handle glass into the mixture. To ensure that this does not happen, Jim twists up the first half inch of the bundle and allows this to cool and act as a buffer between the bundle and the handle.

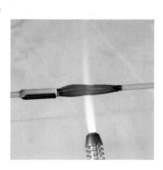

Jim uses two basic motions in mixing. First, there is twisting of the bundle. Here you rotate the two handles in opposite directions. The second motion is what he calls a kinking motion. It is a stretch and helical fold that looks like a heavily twisted towel. He starts throwing this in after about an inch and a half of the bundle is wound up.

He continues this process until he gets to about an inch from the left handle. If he goes further, he chances thermal shocking that joint and losing control. He usually has a clean graphite pad available just in case this happens. Jim makes sure the mass is well mixed by bringing the last bit of the twisted section into the mix by winding it in and mixing it well before pulling the whole mass out.

Fuming

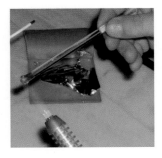

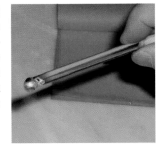

Fuming is the application of metal to the bead surface using the flame. You boil the metal in the flame and it transfers through the air to a warm bead, where it forms a thin coating on the bead surface. Depending on the metal and the amount you apply, this may only affect the glass color (with gold clear turns pink, ivory turns bubble gum pink, black turns peacock green, etc.) or it may form a mirror-like finish on the bead.

Before trying this process, you need to realize that these metallic fumes are very small particles, which will pass through ordinary dust masks or respirators into your lungs. They are not good for you, so you need to avoid breathing them. The best way to do this is to provide good local exhaust ventilation by using a fan to pull the fumes away from your face and out of your workspace. This air movement has to be strong enough that you can see smoke or have smells drawn away from you.

Most glass artists fume gold, but some also fume silver for the earth tones that it imparts to a bead, especially on ivory. Jim uses gold leaf for fuming because he has it readily available for some of his other decorative techniques. This technique, as you will see, is also very easy to do. Try to use only very pure gold leaf to avoid the dangers from impurities such as mercury, which is used in refining gold. A 24-karat sheet of super heavy gold leaf will fume about six beads.

In preparing to fume gold, Jim opens a pad of gold leaf on his work surface and heats up a rod of borosilicate glass to put a ball on the end. He lets this rod cool down until it has lost all of its color and uses it to pick the gold leaf off the pad without scorching the tissue between the sheets. He then marvers and folds the leaf down to where it only covers the bottom quarter inch or so of the borosilicate rod, as seen in the photos to the left. Now he is ready to fume.

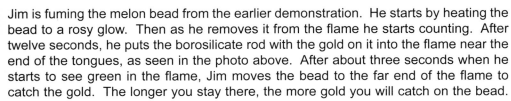

Jim is fuming the melon bead from the earlier demonstration. He starts by heating the bead to a rosy glow. Then as he removes it from the flame he starts counting. After twelve seconds, he puts the borosilicate rod with the gold on it into the flame near the end of the tongues, as seen in the photo above. After about three seconds when he starts to see green in the flame, Jim moves the bead to the far end of the flame to catch the gold. The longer you stay there, the more gold you will catch on the bead.

The bead has to be just the right temperature; too cool and the gold will just wipe off, too hot and it will burn off. In fact, if you get too much gold on the bead, you can usually just burn some off by heating it back up to a rosy glow and holding it there. Be aware, though, that this can make some colors look muddy. You can add more gold by repeating the process. If you only want some areas and not others fumed, spot case the fuming and burn the rest off.

Black-Ended Apple Core Bead

Now let's discuss the construction of one of Jim's signature beads, his black-ended, white apple core, red flower bead. He has been doing this bead since 1993 and it was his poster bead for the 1993 San Francisco Gathering. In these beads he is filling different areas with different colors that go all the way to the core of the bead, in this case black ends and a center of pale lavender transparent over a white core. By Apple Core, he means that the center white section of the bead has that characteristic inward arch that an apple has after you have eaten it away and all that is left is the core. It is really a beautiful and technically challenging bead to make.

To establish the length of the bead, Jim makes pencil marks on the matured bead release at the locations where he is going to place the two black beads, one for each end. He does this, as shown in the first figure to the left, using the drafting compass with leads on both ends that we discussed in the tool section. He sets the opening on the compass to the length that he wants to make the bead and then lightly marks the bead release, being careful not to crack it. These marks will burn off quickly when hit with the flame, so they only serve as a guide for positioning the two black end beads.

In the second photo, we see him making the two pea beads. He winds on glass at the two marked locations and then hits them with the torch flame so that surface tension can round them up into nicely shaped peas.

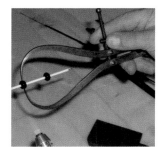

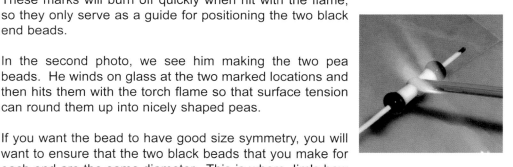

If you want the bead to have good size symmetry, you will want to ensure that the two black beads that you make for each end are the same diameter. This is where Jim's bow caliper comes into play, as we see in the third photo. He tries to visually judge which of the two beads is the largest in diameter and sets the jaws of the bow caliper around the diameter of that bead by squeezing the bow down onto the bead and then adjusting the knurled nut to take up any slack so that the caliper stays in the same place after he stops squeezing.

Then he slides the caliper off that bead without changing its setting and slips it around the diameter of the second bead. If it does not fit around the second bead then that bead is larger and you are faced with the decision whether to make that bead smaller or to reset the caliper to the second bead. Beginners often find it easier to make beads larger so they usually reset the caliper.

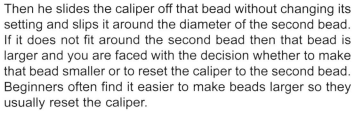

To make a bead smaller, you'd splash a small pool of heat on one side of the bead and touch it with a warm glass rod. When you pull the rod away from the bead some of the glass will be drawn out with it. Pull off whatever you think is necessary to make the bead the right size, and burn off

the thread. Reheat the bead to redistribute the remaining glass around the bead and then measure it again to see if it is small enough.

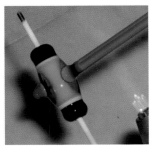

When you measure the diameter of the bead, if there is a gap between the jaws of the caliper and the bead, then it is too small and you will have to add a little glass to make it bigger. Depending how big the gap is, you may want to add another wrap to the outside of the bead or just a few dots of glass and then melt them in to increase the diameter of the bead.

Now that you have the two small round black pea beads for the ends, you have to fill the space in between them with glass, in this case a white core. As you are doing this, you have to make sure that both ends of the bead stay hot enough that they do not crack when you reheat them in the flame. To fill the space, start by heating a white glass rod until it starts to ball and then paint it onto the inner junction between the side of the bead and the mandrel, going all the way around the mandrel. You have to press down slightly as you do this to ensure that you do not trap any air in this junction. Then do the same on the other side. One of these sides will be harder to do than the other because of the old right-left hand-brain-eye thing. This is what Jim is doing in the fourth photo on the previous page.

Then he fills in the middle of the bead to about half the diameter of the pea beads before heating up the whole core. This process is seen in the bottom left photo and then in the two upper right photos on the previous page, we see the apple core shape becoming more visible as the white glass cools. This is a good example of linear surface tension, which causes the glass to form a smooth arc between the two black beads.

Now comes the tricky part. In order to case the white apple core without disturbing the smooth graceful arc, Jim winds a substantial disk of the casing glass around the center of the apple core and collapses it over the core, just as he collapsed a disk to make a round bead. This process sounds easier than it really is because all through this process Jim has to make sure that the ends stay warm enough that they do not crack when he hits them with the flame.

In the third and fourth photos on the right of the previous page, you see Jim building the casing disk at the center of the bead. In the next photo, he begins to heat the disk. In that photo and the first one on this page, you can see that he is mainly directing the flame on the outer edge of the disk so as not to distort the apple core. Every once in a while he will shift the bead in the flame to the right and left to keep the ends warm.

In the rest of the photos on the left of the previous page we see the disk gracefully collapsing inward on itself as it gets hot and spreads out over the surface of the apple core. Notice how the white of the core does not turn transparent until the disk is considerably collapsed. This illustrates how much cooler he is trying to keep the bead. Eventually the core does melt, as in the third photo, but it does not distort because Jim is rotating the mandrel at the right speed to keep everything on center. We see it becoming visible again in the last photo as the white cools.

Now Jim finishes this bead by adding three flower-like decorations onto the center of the cased region. He does not want them to cover too much of the casing because part of the beauty of this bead is its elegant core. He starts decorating by adding three large blue dots equally spaced around the circumference to act as a backdrop, as seen in the upper right photo on the previous page. He melts them into the bead surface in the next two photos.

In the last two photos, Jim adds four coral dots on top of each blue dot, and then melts them into the surface of the bead, as shown in the first photo on this page. Notice how he is mainly heating the dots and not the bead surface. This will help to keep the pattern from swimming around on him.

In the next two photos, Jim goes back and redots each of the same locations with transparent red. This provides some extra variation in the color of the flowers, much like using cased canes does. He then goes back and melts these dots into the bead in the last photo on the left, just as he did for the first set.

Now Jim is ready to distort the bead surface by twisting to turn the dot pattern into a

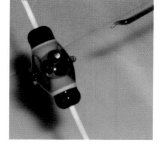

flower-like image. He does this by splashing a pool of heat onto one of the sets of dots and attaching a blue cane into the center of the pattern, as in the upper right photo. When the pool cools to middle red heat, he twists the surface by twisting the cane. Then he lets the bead cool and burns off the cane just above the surface of the bead, leaving a little nub as in the second photo.

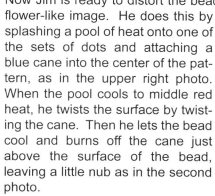

When all three sets of dots are twisted, he heats up the bead to melt in the nubs and to strike the transparent red, flame polishes the whole bead, and flame anneals it before sticking it in the annealer.

Van Gogh Flower Bead

This is one of my favorite Smircich beads. It has a vibrant impressionistic colored flower on the intense short swirling brush stroke background of a Van Gogh painting. To achieve these dynamic variations in color, Jim uses cased canes to cover the entire surface of the bead and then distorts the surface to increase color variation and achieve the swirling brush stroke effect.

Cased canes are smaller diameter glass rods whose cross sections have one color ringing a central core of another color. To construct these cased canes, Jim goes through the process illustrated to the left. He first gathers a ball of the central color on the end of a rod as in the first photo, and lets it cool to set up, as seen in the second photo. Then he paints a thin layer of the second, or casing, color by spiraling it over the surface of the ball as in the third photo. Next he heats up the coated ball and pulls it out into a three to four millimeter diameter cane. He gets such a large cane by making a small flat on the end of his second or punty rod. You see him attaching the punty to the end of the ball in the fourth photo, and pulling it out slowly in the last photo on the left. For this bead, Jim makes four different cased canes, one for the background, two for the flower petals, and one for the stamen area.

With the cased canes complete, Jim is now ready to make the bead. He starts by making a base bead of a light transparent blue, as in the upper right photo. He uses transparent colors because they are stiffer and will help the bead to retain its shape better as he later distorts its covered surface.

Once he has established the base bead, Jim heats it up to get much of the glass to flow out of the ends and into the center of the bead, as seen in the second and third photos on the right. This will make winding the cased cane onto the ends of the bead much easier.

Next he tightly winds a cased cane of opaque red over opaque ivory onto the bead from one end to the other, trying to get each coil to lie right next to the previous one as seen in the fourth photo. Because this cane is fairly thick, he works through the center of the flame. You can see in the last photo on the right how he has completely covered the base bead from one end to the other with the cased cane. If you try this, make sure to make enough cased cane to cover the whole bead. Make multiple pieces if you think you will need them.

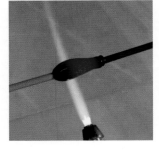

After he has all the cased cane wound onto the bead, Jim makes sure that it is firmly attached to the surface by heating the whole bead up to yellow core heat and then allowing it to cool down again before the next step.

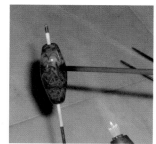

Then Jim distorts the wrapped surface of the bead by splashing on a local pool of heat and twisting small sections at a time with sharp tweezers, as seen in the first two photos on the left of this page. He repeats this process all over the surface of the bead until he gets it swirly looking as in the third photo. This background reminds me of the tie-dyed tee shirts of my youth.

With the background coloration prepared, he now heats the bead, as in the fourth photo on the left, and flows the glass back out into the ends of the bead, one end at a time. As an end develops a bulging water balloon shape, he paddles it out into its final well-puckered shape, as in the last photo on the left.

Now Jim is ready to add the impressionistic flowers to the surface of the bead. He starts with the inner petal cased cane of opaque medium red over coral. To assist in placement of the flowers, he first adds two dots to the bead. One is about one-third of the way down from the top of the bead; the other on the opposite side is about one-third of the way up from the bottom. This puts the flowers on opposite sides and off center from each other. These dots act as targets for the center of the flowers.

Around each of these target marks, Jim applies eight good-sized dots equally spaced on a quarter inch radius circle, as seen in the second photo on the right. He then adds dots of the outer petal cased cane, this one is transparent cobalt over opaque periwinkle blue. These dots are placed slightly radially outward from the inner petal dots as seen in the third and fourth photos.

Jim now melts all of these dots into the surface of the bead in a controlled manner so that they stay in position. He also goes back and reestablishes the shape of the bead using his paddle. When he is done, the bead looks like the last photo to the right.

The dots now have to be distorted to create the shape of the flower. To do this, Jim partially rakes the surface of the bead at each of the sets of dots. He does this by splashing a pool of heat at the location where he wants to distort the pattern, heating up the surface of the bead to a high red heat.

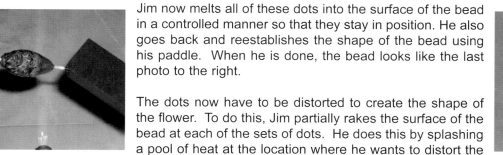

Then he rakes from the inner edge of an inner petal dot to the dot at the center of the flower, as he is doing on the first photo to the left on the next page. The tool with which he rakes the dots is a sharpened cane. In between each rake, as he is heating up the area of the next rake, he sharpens his cane by rolling the point on his paddle, as seen in the second photo on the left on the next page. He rakes each

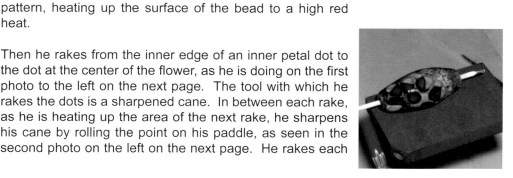

© 2001, James Kervin

27

of the inner dots to the center dot.

When raking like this you want to try to get just the surface hot and not the depth of the bead. Then you slide your tool across the surface of the bead without digging into it appreciably. If you get it too hot and go too deep, you will drag a lot of glass on your tool to the center, instead of just distorting the pattern. Work one dot and then go to the opposite position across the flower pattern in order to avoid getting one area too hot.

After Jim has all of the inner dots raked to the center of the flower, he gives a little swirl to that pattern by heating up the center of the flower to high red heat, touching his cane to the center at medium red heat and twisting it at low red heat, as seen in the third photo to the left.

Now he rakes the outer dots on each petal radially outward from the center of the flower using the same raking technique that he used on the inner dots. Here he is trying to develop a nice star-like pattern. He gets a nice sharp point on the end of each petal by dragging the glass off the surface of the bead with his sharpened cane, as in the last photo on the left. When dragging out these petals he tries to do it in such a way as to fill out most of the surface of the bead, interweaving the petals from one flower with those of the other.

After raking all of the inner petal dots to the center of the flower, Jim will often build up a glass bump there, even though he took great pains to rake shallowly. To get rid of this, he gets the bump hot and double pinches it with his tweezers; first one way and then perpendicular to that to get a purchase on the glass. Then he pulls the excess glass up and out of the bead. If you have a hard time with

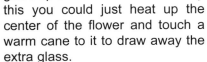

this you could just heat up the center of the flower and touch a warm cane to it to draw away the extra glass.

Jim finishes the bead by adding a little swirl of cased cane to the center of the flower using a cane of medium transparent amethyst over opaque light red. You can see the finished bead in the final picture to the right. Can't you just see Van Gogh painting this bead?

Buttons

Jim's method for making buttons is similar to the method he used to make the shield-like pendant that I discuss in "More Than You Ever Wanted To Know About Glass Beadmaking". He starts out as in the first photo to the left by getting a good-sized gather of glass on the end of a rod. He gets the ball stabilized and pushes it straight down onto the top of his marver, being sure to keep the rod perpendicular to the marver so that the gather will spread out into a uniform disk of glass so that it looks like a doughnut with a rod coming out of it.

Since he wants the button to spread out even larger than this disk, Jim uses a special tool, his split mashers, to squeeze it out even more, as seen in the rest of the photos to the left. He heats up the disk in the flame and pinches it with his split mashers to enlarge and thin out the disk. The short jaw of the masher nestles right up against the rod allowing the long jaw to pinch down onto the top of the disk, as seen in the fourth photo to the left.

Once he has the disk pinched out as much as he wants, as seen in the lower left photo, he shapes the outer surface by rocking and rolling it on his paddle to give it a nice smooth convex shape before decorating it. You could also decorate the button before shaping it but the decorations may get distorted during shaping.

Either way you go, you have to be careful when you decorate the surface not to apply too much heat. If you do, you chance distorting the button. Here you see Jim slowly working some decorative dots into the surface of the button with his paddle. He lightly heats and paddles the dots a number of times before he is satisfied with how far he has them worked into the button. In the fourth photo to the right, you can see the end point. He has left the dots just slightly raised.

Jim wants to twist the dot pattern into a pinwheel, so once he has the dots worked into the surface of the button, he applies a splash of heat to the center of the pattern. When it cools to high red heat, he attaches a cane to it as seen in the lower right photo and as it reaches middle or low red heat, he distorts the surface by twisting the cane. Since a small amount of cane will be left behind on the button when he breaks off the cane, he tries to pick a color that will fit into the pinwheel pattern. You can see the finished decoration in the upper left photo on the next page.

Now Jim forms the shank of the button. He starts by sharpening the cane that he has just twisted the dot pattern with and lightly attaching it to the center dot on the front of the button to act as a punty, as in the second photo on the next page. Then, as in the next photo, he burns off the base

glass rod about a half-inch from the back of the button while holding the button by the punty. He then gathers the remains of the rod into a small ball at the back of the button but does not let it touch the concave surface. He cuts this ball into two with his scissors and pulls the two sides out into two tiny rods about 3/8" long. He then slowly shapes these two tiny rods to form the loop of the shank as seen in the rest of the photos to the right.

The remainder of the process is a little tricky. We see him in the first four photos to the right coaxing these two cut sections into shape to meet at the center, and joining them in the flame. He then shapes the resulting loop with his tweezers and pick until he is satisfied with it.

Lastly Jim grabs the shank of the button with some warmed tweezers and breaks off the cane/punty at the surface of the button by tapping it onto the barrel of the torch. He flattens any remains of the punty using the heat of the flame and a little help from his paddle. Then the button is finished and is popped into the annealer. Because of the large variations in the glass thickness on these buttons, they have to be annealed immediately. Cooling them in vermiculite or a fiber blanket will invariably result in cracking of the button either at the shank or on the face of the button.

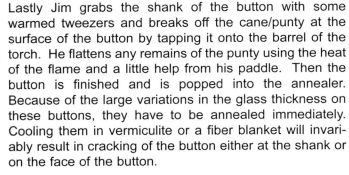

The shank on this button is one of the most secure types because the loop is formed using the rod, which is intimately part of the button. Many other types of shanks suffer from strength problems with the attachment of the shank to the button.

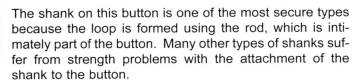

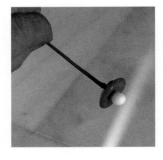

Goddess Pendant

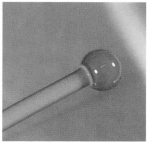

Jim's goddesses are very powerful and moving pieces based upon the prehistoric sculpture "The Venus of Walendorf." It appeals to our deep-seated human emotions.

Jim shares a story about these beads and their mystical appeal. At one bead show a woman came up and told him that she had one of his goddesses and wore it everywhere. She inquired as to whether he had ever made one with a single breast. She said that she had just learned from her doctor that she had breast cancer and there was a chance that she was going to need major surgery. Jim said that he had not but promised to make her one as soon as he got home. Several months later, she wrote and told him that she had worn the bead through all her chemotherapy treatments and that her lumpectomy had been successful. She attributed it to his goddess, but he says that it was really her courage that got her through and he was glad that he could help in some small way. Jim says that he gets goose bumps every time he relates this story.

Jim starts making a goddess by gathering a ball of glass on the end of an ivory rod as seen in the upper left photo. When the ball cools down to medium red, he takes a bite on it with his tile nippers as seen in the next photo. This bite will form the valley on the front and back between the legs that we see in the third photo. He has also attached a small punty onto the end of the legs.

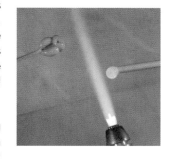

Next Jim burns off most of the original ivory rod leaving about an inch attached to the legs, as seen in the fourth photo to the left. He melts down this rod remnant and flops it forward to form the belly of the bead, as he is doing on the last photo to the left and the top one on the right. In the next photo, we see him poking a belly button into it using his tungsten pick.

In the rest of the photos on this page, we see him grabbing his ivory rod again and making another gather on the end, while keeping the rest of the sculpture warm in the outer reaches of his flame. He cuts this gather in half using his scissors to form the two breasts and heats them briefly to round them out.

In the upper left photo on the next page, we see him heat the rod just behind the breasts. Then he lays them on top of the belly and attaches the back by directing his torch there. At the same time he flexes this joint back and forth applying a little pressure to assure that he develops a good joint. When he has everything attached, he burns off the excess glass rod, leaving the torso, as seen in the second and third photo on the next page.

Then he adds a dab of glass to give the suggestion of a head and forms the neck by running his pick around the base of the head, as shown in the fourth photo to the left.

Lastly Jim adds the loop on which to hang the pendant. This is what he is doing on the last photo on the left and the first two on the right. This loop also provides the suggestion of hair. Forming the loop can be a little tricky. He heats up a small ball of ivory and touches it to the front of the head at orange heat to get a good junction, but waits until middle red heat before starting to slowly draw it out. He draws it out in short segments to form the loop, bringing it around to touch the back of the head.

When the loop is completed, he burns off the extra glass and heats the end to join it. He then works the loop with his pick to refine its shape. You have to be careful as you do this not to have the loop collapse.

Now it is finally time to draw out the legs. He first grasps the head of the goddess with a hot finger tool that he has warmed slightly in the flame. Then he builds up heat in the legs before he starts to slowly draw them out. He directs most of the heat during this operation to the lower half of the legs, so that he will keep nice full hips.

When he has the legs drawn out to his satisfaction he burns off the punty and draws off any extra glass to leave the foot area somewhat pointed. Once annealed, she is ready to wear.

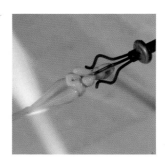